DOWN

WITH

THE

SHIP

BY TOM LEVEILLE

Down with the Ship

Editor : Jeff Hewitt

Cover Art : emma magenta

Book Design : Jeff Hewitt

SFBP First paperback edition

ISBN 978-0-9968350-6-0

San Francisco Bay Press
522 Spotswood Ave C5 Norfolk Va 23517

DOWN

WITH

THE

SHIP

BY TOM LEVEILLE

for Adam.

how does it happen? the seeds you sow. the growing shadows in the room when you're trying to sleep. the kind of nightmares that listen for laughter. that ask for cigarettes on numbered streets. the way you don't want to think about someone chiseling *"whatever"* onto your tombstone. a life once lead where priests might deny you burial on holy land. the past tense of smite. an obituary filled with all the fights you lost. your bedroom turned batting cage. how you went out swinging. the men in your dreams with fists made of lead. the kind that could make an impression on anyone. the allegory of j'adoube. a continuing contribution to the legitimacy of your adjournment. in chess it's called zugzwang. everything spiraling forward when you wish you could stand still. you're atreyu in the swamps saying *"artex you have to fight the sadness."* you never imagined yourself always in checkmate from being blocked by your own pieces.

1

no one can say you didn't try. the weatherman tells you it's going to feel colder than it is. you listen. it's part of your prescription. it's supposed to help. there are detours on your way to work. they're fixing a bridge downtown. something inside you hopes they're making it taller. you've had a hard time being dissociative because the last therapist told you he was *"tired of your shit."* the one before that just liked your money. she'd tell you things like *"bless your heart."* she gave you gold stars. she might as well have been a mortician. maybe she was. there were awards on her wall. to make you feel uncomfortable. she can't just say *"listen kid. these ink blots. they're cats. all of them. they're all dead. you will be too if you keep keeping that picture in your jacket."* she gets it. you stepped in shit a long time ago and you've been checking your shoes ever since. you wake up and check your shoes. you check them before bed. you check them before you check them or whatever. whatever. she spiked your drink with ink and then mailed your parents a stack of rorschach tests from the tallest buildings in town. *"today your child was a crow. a key. a shattered hourglass. two men trying to share the same red bowtie."*

3

you had this epiphany. you bought something off ebay thinking it would make you feel better. it didn't. the return policy's got you guessing more than it should. you were the kind of let down you'd expected to be. you're used to things not working out but now you've got this new found ache to always be somewhere you're not.. you just want to wash your hands. you want to leave them on the kitchen counter and never come back. you wanted to get away from here. and you did. you ended up in baltimore sleeping in a vacant house. well. it used to be a house. before that it was an apothecary. the kind that get the doors kicked in by men with life vests. before that it was a goodwill. maybe that's why you're here. maybe not. it doesn't matter. there are milky white lakes that seethe and warp the floorboards. obviously the windows have been boarded up. the door obviously nailed shut. obviously. you tell all the twenty somethings what the fifty somethings already know. nothing. you keep your damn mouth shut because no one believes in sorcery. at least nobody sober. you want to tell everyone who has never slept somewhere abandoned that when you take a tack hammer to something you step into a time machine. you're a checklist full of junk. how bad the cough is. what lie you choose to blame it on. the narcolepsy. you can't call it time travel. it's cold. someone. maybe you. ripped out the silver lining in everything because they heard you could get a couple dollars for it on light street. it never used to matter. not until all of your things were in a pawn shop. at least you could go and visit at them. watch them call your name as they are dragged down the street into other time zones.

this is what happens when you start blacking out in towns you weren't born in. the vertigo. the hallucinations & holes in your story. the cranberries wrote a song about it once. no one understands that on your way here you tried not to come. that if you stay long enough people will start to nail flyers on you.

7

you forget her name while holding bobby pins. but really. what's there to forget? in the thick of it you check the cupboards. there's no whiskey to put in your coffee. there's no coffee to put in your coffee for that matter. you like her. anyone would. the only thing you can taste is the toothpaste you lost track of. it's lack thereof at four in the morning. you think your mouth is a cathedral in downtown wherever. where everything is hypodermic. where the tooth faerie isn't a joke. where people with habits go to drown. you think about the road trip. a list of cities you got lost in. maybe it's all the smog. the urine in the alleys. that's what really says nothing's wrong with your world. your crusade to find the fragments of what once was. you don't even know what you'd do with them. that's when an ugly aqua chrysler minivan pulls into the royal farms of your memories like a splinter. it's the part of the story where you looked a scar in the face and it looked back. the part where you pretend your family left you in a blue hued parking lot. you remember the church with the blown out doors. how the signs read *"bring your own snakes."* to *"leave your demons at the door."* but these are the kind of demons that have tea in your living room. the kind that know your address. that tuck you in at night. they're so good with names.

9

when everything you step on is a violin. a piano. a song or something like it. always wide open and with its hands out. tonguing wounds. hiding table scraps. spitting out debris like some shitty shipwreck story where the main character is marooned or whatever. there are no natives. only vague markings on a cliff side crag of granite that tell you somewhere in your machine of light and cog work junk and neurons that this has happened here before. it makes you think about the time you thought you were at a funeral. in a grocery store no less. a shopping cart full of things you picked to watch sink. it's not witty or coy anymore. it's just something shiny you want to put your mouth on. you need to make sense of this but everything you're reading is connected to a tangible memory. even some you can't recall having. you remember a grizzled man who looks like he could've played smokey lonesome out of fried green tomatoes on a beach somewhere saying *"listen. we will bury ourselves. you just sing hallelujah."* that is. you think you remember. you think this is what forgetting must be like. that the tv should be quiet even when it's not. that everything dying must be full of song. it's not your god damn job to tell anyone other wise. who are you to ruin that mote of hope.

how did it come to this? maybe she died and you drifted from town to town. maybe she took the keys to your toyota and you decided you never liked that car anyway. it doesn't matter anymore. you miss her but can't describe anything about her to the sketch artist. you go to speak and moths fly out of your mouth. just like in the cartoons. you want to say she looks like the same snowflake fell twice. like that scene from the butterfly effect where evan tells kaleigh *"you were happy once. with me."* you start asking yourself questions that make you sick to your stomach. what will the dog think? why you're upset over things that were never really yours. how come you can't seem to dodge the bullets you saw coming? i've been asking myself for years.

13

somebody bumps into you at a bus stop. you want to say *"watch it pal."* but the person you're looking at doesn't have a face. it's rare that anyone does these days. it's like your heart just can't get out of bed anymore. you'd take this all back but that's predictable. what everyone would see coming. shia labeouf is wearing a paper bag in the basement of your feelings that says *"we are all mongrels."* it only explains what you've always thought. that everyone has something tender inside them but you have to use a knife to get to it. even after all these years when people say they're sorry you've got this knee jerk reaction to say *"it's okay."* even when it's not. your friends tell you to go see someone about these dreams you've been having. you see a man about a horse. you see a palm reader. you start seeing the face of jesus in your soup. so you miss the bus. but did you really miss the bus if you never knew where it was going?

the going away party. no one showed up. you're disappointed that you're disappointed. maybe that's to be expected. some folks make their beds out of catharsis differently than others. you're so jealous of people who never came back up for air. you're crying so the faucets leak out of solidarity. someone asks you why the floor is wet. you look at them like leo is five decks down handcuffed to a pipe. you tell them *"we have been weeping here forever."* it's the dreams. the one you have where your teeth fall out in grated stairwells. or the one you always have where you're at the docks downtown and there's a little girl unmooring all the ships because she thinks she's setting them free. but every time she untied them they just sink. they just sink.

the venn diagram of things that happened to you and things you imagined happened. picture this. she walked away no different than anyone else who said they never would. new pain from an old source. this time you're drifting through the dogwoods with your headphones on. the sixth golden ticket. blood on the ground and is it yours. who dug the the strawberry out of your neck? why'd you come out here looking for a shovel? you aren't really sure what to inter. dizzy from the wasp nest sounds your chest is making you confess. someone killed the thing beating in there. made it grind to an impossible halt. how many "*f words*" it took before she threw up her hands and they stayed there. stuck like song. like molasses. like awful kites scarred to the sky. you made the mistake of making a lot of mistakes. every time you step on the petals you animate them. you're unsure on exactly how deep is deep enough. you just have to keep digging.

19

they say richmond gets under your fingernails. the first place to ever be called *"river city"* in america. today there are "river cities" everywhere. it's like provenance. no doubt they owe their names to the james. fist city. an evolution furnished from fisticuffs. like the first fist to name you. someone reading about it would've said *"it's so bright you can only look away from it."* you recall hearing somewhere that richmond is a place of rolling hills. you want to correct them. you'd say *"richmond knows the way you feel by heart but can't remember your name."* you want to show them your skinned knees.

so they found you in a ditch last again thursday. you tried to help the medicine cabinet lose weight. again. never thought you'd wake up like this. you told them you understand why animals go off to die alone.

none of this makes any sense. you just want people to understand when you say *"the hill i chose to die on had green eyes."* that at dusk you spend all your time cramming light bulbs into your mouth trying to keep the sun awake. to expunge this shadow you cannot step out of no matter how much sunlight you bathe in. everyone knows what happens after dark. with the basic understanding that you are decomposing even as you sit there isn't it a miracle that you're still in love? you think anywhere she lays down flowers is a cemetery. that lately it feels like being at the site where someone tore a building down trying to prove that something stood here once. these hallucinations are only there because you chiseled them out of thin air yourself. you know you're not making any sense of this. you feel like something inside you is on the verge of snapping but unapologetically won't. you want to apologize for being so clumsy. how do you explain that you drag all the days you know you can't have back through the mud. until everything is unrecognizable. until you no longer know who cast the stone that shattered the chandelier in your throat. you're always swapping stories about whose hands came out unscathed. they were never yours. this mess tore your lavender wrists to ribbons. you lied when you said it wouldn't hurt. someone had to make soft this bed of forgotten oaths. this mountain plagued with flowers. how you always wanted to tell her. *"see i've got these shoes. they've got holes in them. i feel everything in them. i wear them when i miss you. if you don't think of me anymore, let me know so i can take them off. i've had them on for years."*

you and all your lost causes. always waiting for the part of the magic trick where what disappeared is brought back. always caught between hell and half way home. most of the time you're just waiting for it to get dark outside. it's like that hotel books song. it goes something like *"either way we decorate this ship it's still sinking."* now every time someone makes a graveyard metaphor you want to show them your bedroom. you can't remember if you read that in the bible or in her texts. it reminds you of the conversation you had about naming children. because. it was the only place she allowed them to breathe. you're always upset about the ghost of who she used to be running its hands over your wounds. about the things you remember most about her. the way she'd say *"i love you."* in the smallest voice. how her thighs would twitch underneath your hands. how she picks at things when she's uncomfortable. it's everything you're not sure what to do with anymore. it's hard you know? opening your mouth without saying something like *"wish you were here."* or *"since you left everything has been covered in knives."*

it's probably because you think about fingertips too much. the legacies they leave behind. how you can only get somewhere if you leave something behind. it's not unreasonable to imagine your impossibly small collection of maps to places you don't go anymore spilling out of your glovebox like tiny white orchids into her lap right? the way she'd look at you like she was covered in blood. like you ruined her favorite dress. it's like you're always trying to turn the ac off when it's already off. you have to put on extra clothes when you know someone's about to say goodbye. it's like that feeling you get when someone says you're special to them but can't tell you why. you always try to laugh it off. the way you can say as a joke that you only eat alphabet soup so you can spell her name in your spoon. it's the little things. they haunt you like perfume when you move too much in bed. there's this man with a banjo on your front porch singing *"son if she didn't come around when you fell apart she ain't comin' around."* and maybe he's right. you've got to stop bothering your mailbox about her. you've got to convince yourself that your bed belongs to you no matter what shapes remain branded into the mattress. you need to turn the sound on your phone off. it's your fault though. for always measuring furniture you know won't fit through your front door. you buy it anyway. because it's perfect. like her midnight miss you texts. like the radio. the way your favorite songs won't let your memories breathe. it's like eating nails for breakfast. like strangers asking if you've lost anything. like they know something you don't.

29

sometimes you fantasize about being thrown through the windshield. to drown out the noise with glass. chanting the mantra of *"someday maybe one day."* you're here but you always felt like you've got somewhere else to be. you just wanna know why lightning can't hit the sands of time. if jesus is coming none of this matters. you've started leaving notes around. like *"where have you been?"* or *"if you need me i'll be at the river smoothing stones by hand."* it's a crisis of faith. the way you think about her changing her mind sometimes. her driftwood smile. all the yellow brick roads you're not allowed to walk down. an exposé on seashell noise. on anything at all. you just want the parts of her that go home for the holidays. you get so upset when you bump into wind chimes. sometimes you think if you repeat yourself enough it will transcend misery and become song. something impossibly red. something you can fall asleep to.

31

there's a town called *"rescue"* close to your home & it's no coincidence that you've never been there.

the sky looks like aged lemon shavings. quiet without the peace. why we do things even when we're told not to. all it does is hurt. the way you've never been in this city before but you swear you grew up in that house. you hate words like *"stay."* and *"please."* it's awful really. that feeling of *"even if i don't, someone is going to cry."* it's always there. it stands in line with you to buy groceries. it likes the cold spot in your bed. it's calculated and clandestine. the way you want someone to say *"make me whole again."* you hope it's not in public. so there's no question of who she's talking to. you don't want to make that mistake. because you know you'll empty out the cupboard in your chest just so she can feel warm. that's just it. how can you hold her hands if they are always filled with stones? nothing you say seems to matter. every *"i miss you"* is just something else she's convinced herself she has to sleep through. you and all your commas. refusing to let anything end. the story always resumes after you've blacked out. but nothing's changed. it's just you. and a litany of stories about picket fences you'll never build. it addles and absconds. all your favorite futures black and placid like an inkwell they refuse to write from. you're always dying to know if the thought of you sleeping next to anyone else makes her sick to her stomach.

35

it's the evening and wisps of sunlight are jutting through dead trees as you drive by. you're always driving by. it's cold in that turn the heat on and back off again every five minutes kind of way. it's crying over roadkill. it's being roadkill. telling children that the animals are just tired and came out to sleep on the asphalt because the sound of passing cars is soothing. it's singing strangers to sleep at bus stops or airports. now it's getting darker and everything is a shadow of something else. what a change of heart. the way people love you until they don't.

37

in a k-mart parking lot in 1994 i walked into a bleeding peach colored tent with orange stripes. to this day i have never seen an uglier thing. the tent looked tiny from outside but once it swallowed me whole i understood. just like everyone does when they are engulfed by the smallest things. i had not wanted to enter this awful unhinged jaw. i had never been to a carnival. i could hear the death trap amusement park rides whine behind me. outside the world was candy apples and laughter. i was lint on the inside of my own pocket. the woman was a fortune teller. there were two murders. one of mouth and one of crow's feet. her lipstick. wounded porcelain. her breath. the business end of an ashtray. turquoise acrylic fingernails and a matching bracelet with an outstretched palm. it looked like my grandmother's hand yet less alive. i watched the two dollars my father gave me disappear into her blouse. her sandpaper voice asked me what my whole name was. she asked me what i came here for. what i wanted to know. i didn't want to be there any longer. so i just said *"just tell me something. anything."* she let out a long sigh and said *"you will never be able to show the people you love that you care about them."* i ran back out to my father. my face still on fire from what she said to me. he didn't ask what happened. i'm sure i wouldn't have been able to articulate anyway. i didn't understand what she meant for many years. they say george orwell changed the future when he wrote 1984. sometimes i wonder what my life would be like had i never stepped foot in that tent. if i would be able to love people any differently had she decided to say anything else to me.

whenever you see a cinder block stuck in the mud at low tide you wonder whose ankles it used to belong to. you want to kiss them and make them better. you'll kiss everything. you wanted to call and tell someone you saw an ambulance today. but then you'd have to explain why you were at the liquor store again. a gray haired man collapsed in line at the register. the paramedics carted his body away. you wanted to ride back with them to the morgue. to have your own place to sleep. instead you bought some brandy & ginger ale. anyway. it was strange to watch someone pass away in front of you. you cried. but it wasn't like when she left. lately you just want to blurt things into her voicemail. you'd say things like *"i get so upset over arizona license plates. i wish i could cut this out of me."* you're afraid of saying something like *"i just want you to be here when the rain stops."* it's hard. doing things people do in someone's absence. you don't like having to wonder. you hate that she wrote *"i'll never give up on you"* on a piece of paper once and then had the audacity to mail it to you. it makes you think about how the back of stamps must taste like goodbye.

41

someone on the internet said *"even the continents came apart."* and you haven't been the same since.

43

the last time she left your bedroom she closed the door so softly you thought you would have to bury it. everything she's gentle with is in a shallow grave in your backyard. you have tiny funerals. you wonder if she will rsvp the day you decide to dig one for yourself. if she will sing hallelujah. lately you confuse her voice with silence. it makes you want to wander at night until you find the place where they hide the sun. if there are street signs you will want to take them down. because. something inside you wants to rename every place you have ever been. it's like you're in one of those commercials from the nineties where someone who loves you jumps out of a birthday cake. like you're a bed she can't remember falling asleep in

45

so you spent the afternoon thinking about the synonyms for betrayal. none of the words were strong enough. how since the last time you held her, it feels like someone took a hammer to your hands. this ache you won't give a name. the bruise you can't explain. the part in the horror movie you cannot look away from. you're a shoebox full of old fists you never gave anyone. everything could've been anything else. it's you saying *"sorry i'm not staring i'm just trying not to blink."* they don't get it. no one does. everything is just too loud and too full of cement and wondering when she's coming home. and there you are. you and jesus. talking about how much cum you have to leave behind. in bodies that aren't her's. the asphalt hell of *"let her go"* and all this whatever. you're thinking about that scene in eternal sunshine of the spotless mind where joel and clem are standing on the ice and he says *"what if it breaks?"* how it's never about what someone did to break something. it's what they do with the pieces when they break it. so what if this whole thing breaks. as long as you don't have to wonder. you're tired of all the people you meet shapeshifting into her the first time they make you smile. it's hard on you. this worn out heart. this gift shop full of excuses. this wedding dance on crows feet. it's like you walked into this store and the only thing they sell are snow globes capturing every moment someone said they loved you and didn't mean it.

47

the mixer. for instance. not the blender in your kitchen. like a speed dating thing. something to pass the time. you're in a squeaking chair. you're all heart murmur and jeopardy. you've gotta keep up with the questions. *"can you make bedroom eyes? do you like black pepper? red pepper? cayenne pepper? how come you don't tell people you're fragile until after they've dropped you? do you apologize before or after you cry? are you good at playing everything is lava? how long can you play dead? can you play the piano without touching it? have you been listening? does this place serve alcohol? do you believe in sorry at first sight? is that the same face you make when the children in your neighborhood ruin your snow with angels?"*

49

a single seagull sits atop a concrete barricade meant to keep the ocean from touching you while you travel toward the tunnel. you think about giving him the strand of hair found in your passenger seat. you wonder if it would understand the sentiment. how do you explain to a bird that you were born an abandoned building? or would he just know. that you never seem to understand why they keep hotel windows locked until you're trying to open them. someone in the distance saying your name. saying *"you can't leave yet. you gotta slow dance to this part."* you've never seen a place this grey. maybe that's why you're still here. why you always end up on rooftops that are never tall enough. why you obsess over bodies of water you dream of drowning in. so what are the great lakes if they cannot flood? if they cannot break their banks and swallow ohio whole. the seagull doesn't weigh in with an opinion when you tell no one in particular that you no longer care if the grass is greener on the other side. you just wanna who woke up all the ditches inside you. why it's always like this when you think about time travel. younger versions of yourself are always trying to show her pictures from when you were happy. it doesn't change a thing. you're always trying to change the last line in all your poems. but she won't let you. maybe if went back you'd lop off your hands so you couldn't write them. if you could go back you would bury disney world by hand.

there's a cliff in town. you heard somewhere that someone jumped from it back in high school. no one talks about it. you woke up one day and it's in your front yard. you'd never actually seen it before. but it's there now. you tell your mother and tells you to pray. you tell your father and he asks you if you want to fishing. you mention it to friends and they change the subject. you want to ask strangers if they can hear that strange and distant ringing too. you don't want to leave the house anymore. not with this thing in your yard. you start thinking every room must be dark with you inside of it. you don't know if the cliff is moving closer to you or if you are moving closer to it. it doesn't matter now anyway. coffee shakes without the coffee. who cares. you're not sleeping anyway. you feel so clumsy. you don't want to talk about it anymore. you woke up this morning and your feet were dangling over the edge. you can't remember how you got here. everything comes to you in pieces. it's so very very still. you remember how relieved someone is when they drop something and realize it wasn't very important when it hits the ground. you wonder if anyone will sigh in relief.

doris on the helplessly large sofa in a pale strawberry living room. the kind of living room you imagine people die in. full of dusty lamps. full of newspapers. how you wound up here to take account of this particular moment was lost several states and handfuls of xanax ago. and there. on that engulfing couch she prattled.

"we're so sick of heaven
round here
it ain't love if nobodies hummin
god's gon' bless you
she went home
well
well
they'll think you're nothin' but a
whatever
i didn't know it was tomorrow
didn't mean to bump into you
not this here
it's okay you jus' gotta wash them hands
it's okay
we jus' gotta get the dirt out
he's gonna try and kill her watch
you watch
why don't you jus' go ahead on
today's my birthday
where's my party hat
i'm scared to death
they call that clairvoyant
don't you miss them call cleo commercials
you 'member that lady's name
did you get my party hat
i told yall about keepin' them doors closed
where you bout to go
home or nowhere
i been tryin'a tell you since you got here
where's my party hat
you don't feel sorry for me
theres nobody down here
theres nobody down here
awful sorry she done you that way"

what a hell of a coming home. north carolina. the war horse hymn. brimming ancient feelings always on the same stretch of road. the catalyst from when you flew the coop. you don't argue with the mirages in the asphalt anymore. the guillotine from your dreams. a death from the finest hewn stone. always driving down dire straits. in the doldrums. you want to know what devils they killed in the hills. where they keep the bodies. if they look anything like you.

57

you used to think that there was nothing more beautiful than the contours of your lovers body bathed in refrigerator light. that was until paul revere showed up on your doorstep out of breath saying *"the sadness is coming."* suddenly you're reminded of things you've forgotten in motel rooms. the feeling you get when you realize it only after driving hours away. a younger you always answering your questions in the form of a question. you just want to slam a door. anything to divert this feeling. this roiling seasick green of the ocean. the toaster in the bathtub of your stomach. this phthisis. overstrung upright iron grand and the grossest diagnosis. ignoring car alarms of *"i would come apart in your arms not to taste someone else's hands."* you just want to put your finger on the pulse of this. it's like razor blades. like rows upon rows of teeth.

a woman walks into the bar and lets the wind in with her. it moves the straw in your long island ice tea far enough away from your mouth that you notice and move it back. she brought november inside with her and you're not wearing a jacket. a bell on the door makes everyone but you turn and look to see who just wandered in out of the dark. she sits down two seats away from you orders an *"i don't care what it is."* something brown with lots of ice in it. topped with a lemon wedge. he doesn't spill a drop. there is so much polished wood between you. so much linoleum. odd conversations and the firecracker sound of people stumbling around a green pool table behind you. you wonder who's telling her to be safe. someone's gotta make sure she wears her seatbelt. but it won't be you. you feel like some stray cat hallelujah. you've always stuck to your guns. you won't say anything to anybody. you won't look at your phone when it goes off. it's not who you want it to be anyway. the bartender asks if you want another one. of course you do. communion for this sermon in a basement. you're supposed to be here. to take account of everyone doing absolutely nothing and living to tell the tale. you were born a jukebox full of second hand smoke. you think about the fire escape. how you'll never take it if this place goes up. in your head you watch everyone else explode towards the door. smoke detector singing their unpalatable songs as you lock the door behind them. in your head you return to the smoldering licorice finish of the bar and sit down with your drink. but the building isn't on fire. it's just two o'clock in the morning and your imagination is gluing feathers to anything trying to call it an angel.

a thousand names for rummaging through the garbage to stay alive. unsuspecting aunts feeding neighborhood cats with craters for footsteps in the lawn. elements of the subconscious turning men in trenchcoats into lumbering things on the edge of town. old legends asleep in our fathers tongues. special segments on the history channel. giorgio tsoukalos weighing in on the disparaging nature of cultures that cannot procure proof of nonexistence. perhaps better known as bigfoot. the superstition that surrounds it existed long before its name. scientists say people have always needed a *"larger than life"* creature to exist. the skunkape. the sasquach. the skoocooms. pejoratives. the kind of thing that transforms nearby tree lines into sensationalism. inherent needs to answer questions that remain unexplained. the tireless sportscaster review of frame 352. the turn radius of bipedal creatures at a given gate and pace. the need of local lore and townsfolk taking to the forest with pitchforks. disillusioned acclamations of noises in the night. hometown hoaxes. naysayers. all the way back to the beginning. thomas wanting to put his fingers in the wounds.

here's how it happens. the morning after. you reach into the drawer where your t-shirts live and find it austere. you shrug because you don't really care. you can't remember when last it was you had something to whet your whistle. or how long it's been since you made the carpet upset. who wouldn't be? the contents to the upended ashtray strewn around the apartment look like the smallest war to ever take place in norfolk. some midnight thief must've made off with the lighter because it isn't in any of your favorite spots. maybe you chucked it. along with anything else that makes noise when it lands in the neighbor's yard. you don't remember putting the refrigerators belongings in the bathtub. or that someone maybe you scrawled a buzzard on the bedroom door. then again who would? you'll pretend it's spring again before putting on your winter coat. you go out with an unlit cigarette in your mouth hoping for a stranger to bum a light from. or drag yourself to the corner with couch cushion change to buy some fire. on your way you won't bother looking back. another day on eggshells. another november choking on birthday candles. on your way home you'll step over beer cans. the kind you fell in love with. you'll wonder who had the last laugh last night. or if beer tastes the way her sweater feels in your hands.

the phone rings. you answer. the sound of your own voice cracking the first time you begged her to stay bounces through the receiver.

you lied when you said it didn't hurt. you think someone would be happy to sit next to you while you waste your twenties away. at least you've still got something to throw away. smoke heavy air splinters light into shards you can hold. the jukebox got on you like sweat. you listen in on someone on a payphone trying to talk over the music. that's what love must be like. and there you are. constantly inconsistent. you think mercy must be measured in liquor. you wonder if you could get frequent flier miles for loving things that leave.

65

you know the car will crash and how. you're paralyzed in the moments leading up to impact. you live to tell the tale. wrote a poem about it. everyone's glad you made it. there. you did it. you made a metaphor. so some stranger or family member can understand now. everything's clear when you tell them it was a massacre. you really liked that car. you gave it a name. you tell them you don't know how to explain that you saw it coming other than reminding them about the time their dog took off toward the street and they tried to call for it but couldn't because of that lump in their throat. they loved that dog. all they could do was watch.

67

the road has made you weary. you call a random number in your phone. jack picks up. gonna smoke till he dies. he tells you the same stories every time you talk. they're classics. he's jeopardy without the questions. knows a couple things about a couple things. he talks to cicadas. the tip of his ear is missing. says it's from a fist fight he barely survived. skin of his teeth. remembers his shipyard job. courier. bicycle bearer of bad news. the gas wars. lowest he recalls was allan's automotive. seventeen cents. charlie english's five & dime. eighteen cents. he remembers taking to the town with the top down. just him and some tall boys. says back then you could sit em right in the passenger seat.

eleven o'clock & homeward bound on the twenty towards florence. only you and the radio. you feel like a heart transplant. nothing but pine trees. nothing. there are no stars. a rust colored lincoln going ninety surges past you on the shoulder with no lights on hitting the the woman in the lane next to you. there are children in her car. and then it happens. you feel them welling up inside you. some uncountable number of impossibly white rabbits in a wide eyed panic explode into hysterics as though under the duress of fangs. he yanks the wheel and collides with the guard rail in front of you. some folks say time slows down just before impact. others say it speeds up. when asked to recollect you'll say you couldn't tell the difference. just like everything in your life you swerve to get out of the way but it's not enough. you wake up to sirens. paramedics weigh in on how lucky you are to be here. everything is a blur. the next day in a rental car you drive past your own skidmarks. you can only think about david. man who caused the accident. how he lost an incisor. you remember wanting to search his floorboards for it. to steal it. to keep it in your pocket. forever.

71

the feeling of cars rushing by on the turnpike. that
feeling of falling. sunblock to stay inside your house.
someone always someone on the radio doing a plug
for the newest dating app reminds you strangely of
shakespeare. dogs. cry whatever & let them slip.
lately you've got the quakes. the *"never noticed until
someone told you"* shakes.' this longing you
absorbed through reverse osmosis. skinner's theory
on intermittent reinforcement. the year of the
neighbors conjecture. the *"yeah someone's in there
but nobody's home."* the winter you remember the
electric bill. how the longer you left the lights on the
more certain you were that she'd come back. you're
the embodiment of diminishing returns. it's like you
fell in the forest and ever since you've been asking
people if they heard it.

staring leads to fucking.

you want to know why telemarketers only call when you're crying. how people got inside the radio. a cruel game of charades where you show someone you love them but they can't guess what it is. the way things are the worst when you're certain they're perfect. pigeon superstition. so you flipped a coin once. heads says *"don't kill yourself."* tails says *"i'll pray for you."* the problem is the coin landed somewhere out of sight. see also: schrödinger's cat. your heart is just the way she left it. your friends talk about sneakers the way you talk about being married. what an axe to grind. when you think about it you want to make the noises people make when they're explaining to mechanics what's wrong with their cars. sometimes you forget you're not alone. this is one of those times. now you're a dead battery or a carburetor in front of ostensible acquaintances. people are looking at you so you have to change the subject. you blurt out the first thing that pops into your head. *"do you ever wonder if the mail man misses you on sunday?"* they only look at you stranger. when you can't take it anymore you do your best man impression and leave. it's like the music stopped and everyone was looking for a chair. you can't look at the sky anymore without getting some of it on your face.

you're an archeologist now. you've always obsessed over rubble. ground zero. you are paparazzi to an impact crater. technology is fancy these days. a scrap of victorian wallpaper. the last inhabitants welcome mat. the refrigerator door. your masterpiece. alphabet magnets still spelling *"wish you were here."* you're reminded of lazarus. you wonder if jesus wandered through his body before waking him up. you think of how this debris will end up in the lungs of passers by. you look up and notice you're no longer alone in the alcove. a bearded twenty something looks at you and says *"i didn't think rich kids came into this neighborhood to get high."* he asks not to have his picture taken. volunteers information that makes you uncomfortable. can't remember how he got here anymore. tells you he's sure that if you say baltimore slow enough it sounds like hallelujah. says the junk took all his friends. says it's like church but everyone's a pallbearer gesturing to an abandoned house across the street he tells you *"i found a photo album in there. sometimes i pretend the people inside it are my family. that there is someone out there that misses me."*

you want to bruise yourself into honeycomb. you'll placate the neighbors by saying *"it's not for the juice. or the squeeze."* you tell your audience of green grass to hold the applause. there will be no clapping until you are more wasp than hummingbird. you tell your lawn you earned this. and maybe you have. so for this type of roulette you need more than one player but it's hard to get people to play if there's no way out. you can't just explain that everyone dies at the end. so consider this dissonance. for instance: you come home and mel gibson is yelling *"freedom"* in your living room. he's been yelling in your house forever. you think *"so this is what i unhinged my jaw for?"* it's like you told this joke and no one heard it. then someone else repeated it louder and everyone laughed.

you are blue with fishhooks from chumming the waters. someone's watching you pick at the spot where a scab used to be. you tried to explain it in a poem but that only made things worse. it's all a neologism for something. you get dirt on it and give it a new name. everything's always in a strange vernacular. you don't argue semantics over what was once your bedroom is now called *"the crying place."* everything's under some strange enchantment. it's why you watch horror movies. why you make collect calls. you're still giving things new names but the dichotomy remains the same. a new layer of ash. in your version of the story you were reaching for the life raft. in theirs you swam until you couldn't see land and gave up.

83

sometimes you're the car and it's someone else's job to talk you up. the only thing they can say is *"please."* sometimes you're the car salesman and you have to show strangers what's under the hood and it makes their daughters cry. *"listen. listen. the color of champagne could make anyone carsick."* now you're on this game show and the answer to every question is *"i never thought i'd end up this way."* after the commercial break it's another round of *"last one to remember when or why they ever left their house in the first place wins."* but the games stacked against you because the first question is about your father and all of your answers are already in tears. there are no laugh tracks. they just roll the credits, a list of wounds that know your last name. that girl with the ouija board skin. the one whose body language you shoulda never read. the chain smoker who thought your asthma was cute. every hospital within a fifty mile radius. every person who's ever said hallelujah. hallelujah.

you heard it & you heard it & you heard it but your throat. cicada filled & jilted. lilting & refusing to breathe. this new phantom limb syndrome where you wake up thinking she's still there. your ghost town mouth & the summer every stranger passed by you so close. the night you tore out your shoulder trying to open the world inside a bottle before taking a claw hammer to it. summer of soft & lofty. pissed & dismissive. the summer you tried to have an unorthodox relationship with girls who only spin for the music box. summer she led you through the dunes with both hands soberly holding yours saying *"hurry. you've got to hurry."* summer she cropped you out of photos for instagram. lorazepam & cradling brown bags over it. her imagination the butcher shop in your home town. the summer you slept in your car on nebraska avenue. before you wore a floral pocket t-shirt with trying to flip the hourglass filled with baby teeth. the summer you wore your thumb out on the highway and disappeared in a cloud of feral cats. the time summer almost made you a basket case. though you can't remember the dd/mm/yyyy of the incident. was it the summer of throw back thursday? or the foo fighters with the top down you can never tell. summer you were down there with the tears in your eyes. summer you hemorrhaged light & confessional tone. summer of going places alone. the summer you sank the whole god damn ship. the summer you said you'd never share. but you did. you did.

87

you stepped out into the sunlight and saw your shadow. six more weeks of sadness. it's always like this. you know what a bindle is without having to google it. it reminds you of all the times you thought of a comeback to something upsetting someone said to you two weeks after it happened. you feel like an explosion in the distance. it's not unreasonable. you're capable of anything if you could just get out of bed.

unpacking the narrative. you want to know why i drove to ohio and so do i, why i thought georgia could save me. why they burnt atlanta to the ground. never liked peaches or pennsylvania to begin with. so this dance this barefoot black tracks through the backyard of where i said i'd leave you but never could. twisted precious pressure amen and ankles and who tied the cinderblocks to mine. who taught me how to swim. can i even tread water? bound by magic tricks i spent nights in knots believing were real. so who are the poems about. how many times have i lied. whose hair was in the shower drain. black or brown. paper or plastic. which hotel. what city. whatever. who put the bleeding earth in your hands. it wasn't me. why chesapeake keeps tabs on me. the real questions. momentum. lack thereof. you know i sob to freyr by peter broderick. i also sob to songs that sound like freyr by peter broderick. in gusts of wind that remind me of your voice. i can't control it these days. my heart gets dressed up in its ugliest easter egg pink. the soft parts exposed. like changing tires on interstate in february. so i still never told you how black her hair was. why she never told her parents or why i did tell mine. is that why you've come to the edge of the world. to sweat and to swear at old photos. i have to prove you existed. you're more tangible in a story than in my arms. you had the chance to kiss me in the rain and didn't. someone's asking how. how'd you get all these holes. we got away from the point again. here goes. nothing. my bottom of the sea impression. coughing up whatever. someone went missing. i imagined hanging posters on telephones poles in town but cropping you out of the picture. it's just our hands. our accidental everything. only you would recognize the moment. it was the day everything came apart. the day i fed randy in cincinatti. though we drove away in a hyundai. he cried. i cried. you didn't. would you remember the way our fingers locked together. i wondered how you let me go. it was calculated. i calculated empty chairs at holiday dinners. the aftermath. you know i measured the difference by distance. georgia and ohio. the day i drove to dayton and back again. where i was going. why. what it meant. how unrequited you became. i became a drifter. wandering for warmth. you became a music box. i became something else. the life or death aesthetic. the way you hang up phones. the planets aligning. can you feel the dance in your feet yet. or why your car keys are in your hand. me either. i cling to all the wars i know i'll lose. the absence is its own absence. i was so close to you that i couldn't see you. and this is just the beginning. the preamble. wrapping up the loose ends. the string on my jacket i won't cut off. how i never loved anyone as much as

About the Poet

Tom Leveille is a 29-year-old non binary spoken word artist hailing from Newport News, Virginia - born and raised. Leveille studied at Old Dominion University but did not throw a hat into the poetry scene until very recently.

They discovered the world of poetry and spoken word through Twitter. Tom owns and operates the legendary @avxlanche account, which since August 2014 has exploded to over 55,000 followers and growing. They are also active in the community as a staunch member of Slam Richmond leading writing workshops, and cohosting the weekly slam/open mic.

A Richmond slam champion, a writers den slam champion, College Unions Poetry Slam Invitational 2015 Sacrificial Poet, Southern Fried 2016 competitor, and Texas Grand Slam 2016 competitor Tom has, in addition to this collection, published a chapbook through Impossible Wings Press entitled "the year no one said hallelujah." Their work has been featured in various places including altdaily.com, samueljay.co.uk, and the pulp zine.

Recently branching out as a touring poet, Leveille is slated to perform at over a dozen colleges & slams across the Atlantic seaboard in the spring of 2016, with another tour spanning the entirety of the south: from Virginia to Arizona and back.